CONNECTIONS

DEDICATION

This book is dedicated to my son, Kenny Lindner (6/23/1983 – 5/14/2002)

And to the members of my local Writing Group. Without this group and their continued support, encouragement and feedback this book may never have become a reality.

CONTENTS

INTRODUCTION

This book is a compilation of verses which have been written over several years. It has been written with the intention of connecting humanity with spirituality through nature in order to bring Peace, Hope and Inspiration to others.

It was so warm last night that I did not pull my shades down. I could see the sun starting to come up, so I took my cup of tea out on to the sun porch and sat in my white wicker rocking chair watching the new day dawn. As the birds awoke, they started signing me a symphony getting louder with more sounds every minute. I could look up through the skylight and see the high clouds gently floating by. As I sat there in total peace without a care, I thought this is one of the things I will miss about living here. It has always been my favorite thing to do .... to watch the sunrise, journal and exercise on the sun porch before starting my day. Then my mind drifted to wondering how I will start my day in my new house. So many rituals developed here, but exciting to think of the new rituals I will discover. A robin has just landed on my railing as if to say 'look at me - you too will soon be free to fly carelessly wherever your heart takes you". Watching the wind patterns on the water, the creatures of the pond playing carelessly in their world, the sunlight constantly changing the landscape as it dances with the trees ..... these memories will linger as they are replaced with new experiences. To be able to sit and contemplate all that is around me, to explore new surroundings, develop new friendships this is what lies ahead for me. An exciting new life where I can take the peace, serenity and stillness that is now within me whatever my future holds.

2014 REFLECTIONS

Another year has flown by
Where did the time go?

One war ends, another begins
Recovery from natural disasters continue
Weather patterns change
People are homeless
People go hungry
This paints a dismal picture
Yet, there is hope.

People will suffer
Compassion heals
Feelings exist
Understanding allows them to pass
Criticism and judgments hurt
Awareness and acceptance brings
harmony.

Where love resides
Hope exists
When hope exists
Peace will grow
When peace grows
Beauty is seen
When beauty is seen
Life is full of joy
When life is full of joy
It is a pleasant place to be.

May this coming year be full of
Love
Hope
Peace
Beauty
Joy
And a pleasant one.

MY FIRST HURRICANE WALK ON THE BEACH
Ocean City, NJ

Driving south to where two hurricanes are
predicted to hit land
I ask myself: "What am I doing?"
After the 9 hour drive
The GPS guides me to the destination.
Tonight is not the time to walk the beach
Heavy rain, strong winds, no one is out and
about.

The restaurant in the hotel is closed
I venture out in search of food
Drenched in minutes
Wind fighting my leg movements
A store is found.

Back to the hotel
Barely able to hold onto the bags
Dry clothes, hot tea and salad
Thank heavens for no more driving tonight.

Fit-full sleep mixed with joy
The sound of crashing waves
The howling wind
The smell of salt air
My body vibrating with the hurricane's
energy
Sleep comes and goes.

The new day dawns
Daylight slowly arriving
The hurricane blocking the sun
The beach beckons me.

3

Hot coffee
Hot shower
Peanut butter crackers for breakfast
Dressed for the storm
Out I go.

It is easy walking with the wind
I am drenched within seconds
The wind so strong it is blowing the sand
I cannot see the beach
Yet it is solid under my feet
The wind creates art work in the sand
Making beautiful designs
That can be seen if the wind stops for a
moment.

The horizon is no longer endless
As the hurricane's front meets the sea
There is no separation between worlds
We are all one
All connected.

I am awake
I am alive
I am clear
I am free
I am here now.

Waves break out at sea
Waves break closer to the shore
Waves break closer to me
The wind curls water off the tops
The tide is coming in
Threatening to touch my feet.

I am alone on the beach
Sea gulls rest in the sand

4

Sand pipers scurry around
Off in the distance a bulldozer hums
Moving beach sand
Creating a buffer
As the high tide approaches.

Past the bulldozer I walk
To the point where the sea meets a sand
dune
Time to turn around.

The pink hotel can barely be seen
The rain feels like little daggers hitting my
face
I am getting sandblasted
The roar of the ocean is deafening
My foot steps in the sand have disappeared
Leaving no trace of me
Water is running down my pants
Filling my shoes
My feet are warm and comfy
Surrounded in bamboo socks.

Breathing in is easy
All I have to do is open my mouth
The wind forces fresh air into my lungs
Breathing out takes effort
As it must overpower the force of the wind
How strange to be so conscious of my
breathing.

The incoming tide forces me closer to the
dunes
The sandy beach disappearing
The high water markers no longer visible
Waves splash up onto the pier of the
boardwalk

No need to do my exercises
Walking into the wind is a workout
When the wind gusts
I have to stop and brace myself from getting
blown over
The hotel is near
I am finally there.

I am safe, protected and dry
Sitting here in my hotel room
With pen in hand
Paper in my lap
Eyes glancing out to sea
Simply being present.

My mind wanders to home
My little house on Lake Parker
Nestled among the Green Mountains of
Vermont
In the corner called the Northeast Kingdom.

It feels small, secluded, confining
Almost claustrophobic
My heart belongs to the ocean
I am calm and at peace
In the midst of this hurricane
I feel free
No longer afraid
The world holds endless possibilities
Anything is possible
Once you make up your mind to do it.

The ocean is washing away all that no
longer serves me
Restoring my courage to move on
My adventurous spirit has returned
Thanks to this journey into two hurricanes.

6

As I was walking the beach
Thoughts of God came to me
God is not a single man
God is simply a name, a word
That we humans attach to something larger
and more powerful then all there is
God is within each and every one of us
All we have to do is go within to discover it.

What brought me here at this time
Is a bereaved mothers conference
Sponsored by Umbrella Ministries
My walk on this path of grief
Has been a solo journey right from the
beginning
There were no family or faith to guide me
I sat with my grief
I embraced my pain
My heart ached
Paralyzing me
Yet, I continued to breath, to walk, to live.

This morning while walking the beach alone
I finally understood how my only child could
leave this physical world
We are so small
This earth is so small
It is restrictive, confining and claustrophobic
When compared to all there is
There is so much more than our eyes can
possibly ever see.

Before I turned around
I knew there was more
I just couldn't see it
It is that knowing that Kenny could see
When the time came

7

He freely went with courage, strength,
knowing and no looking back
He didn't want to die
Yet he knew that this physical world was
too restrictive for him to reach his potential
He reached out and took the hand that was
offered
Simply because he could
Because he knew the time had come
To go beyond the physical restraints
To explore the vast unknown
To become part of all there is
To be one with "God" In all it's glory
Beyond the boundaries that humans create.

I, as Kenny's mother, will always miss him
There will always be a sadness within my
heart
While at the same time my heart feels
Joy for being Kenny's mother
Blessed that he is my son
Proud that he choose to take that hand
To be part of the greater good
To expand his horizons
To always be connected with all there is
I am thankful for the many gifts he gave me
during his physical life time
And for the many gifts he now shares with
me.

We are all like the water blowing off the top
of a cresting wave
Part of the sea one moment
Becoming free with the wind
Only visible for a second or two
Then returning to the sea.

If we are not aware
If we do not see
If we do not appreciate what is right in front
of us
We will miss this magical moment
This beautiful gift that is given to all who
simply pay attention.

THE BLOOD MOON

A full moon
A harvest moon
A blood moon
A total eclipse.

A magical event
Happened 33 years ago
Will happen in 18 years
You may only see it once in your lifetime.

The time was early enough to stay awake
The sky was clear
The night was cool and crisp
The moon was visible from my front deck.

The night sky was full of twinkling stars
More than I ever remember seeing
So close they were almost touchable
The milky way was massive
Creating amazing paths.

The moon's movement was visible to the
naked eye
A huge ball in the sky
Slowly disappearing
Transforming into an orange ball.

The energetic pull drew all that no longer
serves me from my body
My heart expanded
My body relaxed
My mind emptied.

My very being was mesmerized

I was safe
I was held by all there is
Endless possibilities exist.

The power of this event
The magic of this night
Connecting all that exists
Aligning all there is.

The nourishing sun
The thriving earth
The mystical moon
Coming together in perfect symmetry.

No human intervention
Nothing to do other then be aware and
observe
Appreciate this natural event in all its
beauty
With love flowing from our hearts.

ON BEING DIFFERENT

Being married is normal
Having children is normal
Having grandchildren is normal.

The death of a child is different
The death of an only child is different
Having no surviving children is different
We are different when our child dies.

Shock, denial and pain
Having no direction
Living without your child
These become your new normal.

Death of a child defies all logic
It makes no sense
No bandages can cover your wounds
Nothing can relieve your suffering.

Friends no longer know what to say to you
You do not know what to say to them
Innocent questions from strangers become
triggers
Normal conversations are painful
reminders.

Your wounds are ripped open time after
time
Insulating and isolating yourself from others
Only increases your burden
Your world is no longer a safe place.

One day leads to the next
One week passes by

One month disappears
Another year has ended.

The wound becomes less raw
The scar tissue runs deep
The void within remains
You learn how to cope.

You are still different from what was normal
You meet other parents who share your
difference
You are not different from them
You discover a new way of being.

Yes, you are different
Your world was shattered
It will never be the same.

You finally find the courage to say:
"I am different "

CHRISTMAS LOON
2015

Winter was late in arriving this year
Keeping the waters of Lake Parker open
Allowing the loons time to linger before
migrating south.

Four days after Christmas a pair of loons
landed
To rest, to fish and to spend the night
They were a wonderful gift
Bringing joy, appreciation for nature and
love of all living creatures
Reminding us of summer days gone by.

That night, temperatures dropped
By morning the lake was freezing
The open water disappearing
The loons were still fine
They needed to leave soon
A flock of geese were along the shore in
front of my house
They took off as soon as daylight dawned.

The pair of loons continued to fish
They kept swimming around
Keeping their little patch of water open
Around noon, they both tried to take off
One made it
The other did not
He hit the edge of the ice and went no
further
The one loon kept circling, calling to the
remaining loon.
Eventually the calls stopped.

14

The loon kept trying to take off
He just couldn't make it
The loon panicked
The water kept freezing
The loon became exhausted
Emergency calls were made
Those that answered could not help
Night started to set in
Darkness engulfed us all
We were all sure the loon would be frozen
in the ice by morning
Prayers were said.

As a new day dawned
The loon could still be seen
Contentedly fishing
Continually swimming to keep the water
open around him
A flock of geese landed on the ice
They did not come near the lone loon.
He tried to take off
Only to land on the ice
He waddled back to the open water.

The VT loon specialist was finally contacted
He said to monitor both the loon and the
ice
He would come rescue the loon if necessary
A cold water rescue team was contacted
They only had a skeleton crew due to
Christmas
They would come do a training exercise
But needed to wait till they were back up to
full staff
In the meantime, all I could do was wait and
monitor.

15

An ice auger was borrowed to check the
thickness of the ice
A cage was borrowed to safely carry the
loon
Temperatures started to rise
Long range weather predictions looked
good
The loon was safe for now.

Predictions changed
Below zero temperatures would quickly be
upon us
If the loon did not leave, a rescue would be
necessary
He had one more day
Saturday morning arrived with bright
sunshine
The loon looked like he was testing the
open water without trying to take off
He would then swim back to the other edge
and try again
He appeared to be trying to figure out how
to take off
There was not even 20 feet of open water
remaining
Loons need 3 times that much to take off
After watching him for most of the morning
I turned from the window to do some work
The next time I looked
He was gone
I stood and watched
Getting my binoculars to check the entire
lake
He never reappeared
He was nowhere around
He had to have figured out how to take off.

16

My neighbors called to say the Benedictine
Nuns were praying for the loon
They had a contact who would come rescue
him
Amazing how at the time of all their prayers
He managed to fly away
On the wings of angels
With the help of divine intervention
This was certainly a miracle of nature.

The story of this loon ends well
Not all stories have happy endings
Life goes along and all is well
Then in a moment of time
Tragedy strikes
Our lives as we knew them are lost
We are left alone
Panicked, exhausted
Not knowing where to turn for help
We rest, we figure things out
While help awaits
When the time is right
We can once again soar
To continue to live our lives
Trusting we are never alone
Hanging on to hope
Most importantly
Never giving up.

REFLECTIONS OF
2015

When your only child dies
What remains is a deep dark hole within
you
Where once there was light, joy and love.

That hole draws you in deeper and deeper
It is easier to go to that dark place
Then to face the living world around you.

The rest of the world continues along
Bringing constant reminders
Of all that you no longer have.

Time marches on
Secondary losses come along
As difficult as these are
They are easy by comparison.

Physical possessions remain
Memories remain
Love remains.

Every new day dawns
Another day without your child
The struggle to not fall into that hole
continues.

Some days are easier than others
Some days are easier to fall into the hole
Yet every day dawns.

Shifts slowly begin to occur
As you create your own road map of life

18

Grief is replaced with wanting to be more
than just a grieving mother.

That deep dark hole still exists
But is replaced by a cloud of sadness and
depression
You still do not know how to navigate this
new road of life.

You attend a Bereaved Parent's Conference
for the first time
You attend an Umbrella Ministries
Conference for the first time
You take a journey south by yourself
Visiting the first place where your child
went without you
You stand on the pier where his picture was
taken
You walk the beach where he had walked
You attend a Courage and Renewal
Conference
You attend a meditation retreat.

All these things you do by yourself
Believing you are alone
You meet other grieving parents
You meet other people who do not shy
away
In their stories you find understanding and
compassion
Hope and inspiration grows.

Strangers stand by your side
They hold your hand
They share your tears
They lovingly hug you.

Courage begins to surface
The cloud begins to disappear
You realize you do have something to offer
The road map of life becomes clearer.

My road map has been developing for over
13 years
My path was a solo journey
No family or faith to guide me
People would tell me I couldn't do this
alone
My first thought was always I am doing this
alone
Who are you to tell me I can't?

There is help out there
There are people who care
No one has to walk this journey alone
They only need the courage to show up.

MISTY MORNING

The sun is rising earlier
Bringing more day light hours
Temperatures are rising
Bringing signs of spring
Mud season has arrived
Bringing challenging driving conditions
Deck chairs start to appear
Allowing a beer to be drunk in the sun
The lake is starting to melt
Looking like a patchwork quilt.

Morning mist is rising off the water
Clouds hang low and heavy while holding
the rain
The two masses gently touch each other
Morphing into one
Air gently moving
Creating continuous change.

Two separate spheres merge into one
One rising from the earth
One lowering from the sky
You can see it
You can feel it
Yet you cannot touch it
Always shifting and changing
Here one minute
Gone the next
So much beauty
With no clarity
No definition
No boundaries
A natural phenomena
Created without human involvement.

Two worlds coming together
The physical world
The spirt world
Always present
Always connected
At times they feel separate
So far apart
At times they merge together
Becoming one
Constantly changing
Constantly flowing
Simply being.

A misty morning
Bringing the gift of magical connections
Between two worlds
Becoming one.

SPRING EQUINOX

Clocks have been changed
Sap is running
Boiling has begun
Smells of maple syrup fill the air.

Heavy winter clothing tucked to the back
Ice cream stands start to open
Snow disappears
Ice melts from the lakes.

Birds begin to sing
Birds migrate north
Four Canada Geese seen in a cornfield
The first flock fly overhead
Landing on some open water
Milk shakes are enjoyed while sitting on a
bench along the shore
While watching loons playfully swimming.

Spring brings warmth, hope and new
beginnings
A new man enters my life
Sparking something deeply hidden within
Is romance possible?
Am I ready to love again?

Another cold snowy night
The moon is days away from full
In the middle of the night
The brilliance wakes me from sleep.

Too cold to get up
Too dark to see clearly
The moon brings light to the dark
The warmth of my inner light

Meets the moon light.

The Spring Equinox is a powerful time
Bringing new energy
A time to transition from dark to light
From cold to warmth.

Shedding layers of clothing
Releasing all burdens
A time to grow
A time to flourish
A time to be seen.

A new day dawns
With brilliant sunshine
A new beginning with endless possibilities
Daylight allows us to see clearly
To go forward with hope
To allow our inner self to blossom
Like the new buds
Trusting our unique beauty.

To spread our wings and soar
Like the birds migrating north
To rest in joy
To be playful in the waters of life.

To trust our inner wisdom
To open our hearts to love
To begin anew
With the Spring Equinox.

HAMPTON BEACH

It is 1999
I come home from work to find a note from
Kenny:
Ryan and I have gone to Hampton Beach
Turbo is with us
Spending the night
Be home tomorrow.

Independent and free
His love of the ocean
Took him there.

Every Mother's Day weekend I would
escape to the ocean
Stopping here in the RV for breakfast or
lunch
Maybe just driving through
Never walking the beach.

Today I come here to walk the beach with
you
To feel your presence with me
To walk where you had walked
To let thoughts of you flow through me
To hold you in my heart.

So many footsteps in the sand
None of them yours
Mine will disappear with the tide.

The ocean meets the sky
The ocean touches the sand
Billowy clouds high above

Sea gulls fly overhead

Sand pipers run in the sand.

Pieces of green sea glass catch my eye
Into my pocket they go
Green represents the color for the heart
The pieces represent my broken heart
I can pick up the pieces
I can keep on walking.

The pieces will never fit together again
You will never walk by my side again
You will always walk with me
You will always be in my heart.

We are like the sand and the sky
Joined together by the ocean
One step at a time
Walking by myself
Never alone
You are always with me.

YOU'RE NOT HERE

I loved you before you were conceived
I carried you inside me for 9 months
I held you
I nursed you
You slept on my chest
I loved you more with each passing
moment.

I was your mother
You were my son
We were so much more
We had a special bond
That could never be broken by time.

You left my side to go off to college
You were on your way home to be back at
my side
You made it home just not to me
You no longer stand at my side.

I walk where you have walked
I drive on roads where you drove
I do things that you have done
I see sites that you have seen.

I go places where you have been
You are no longer there
You are not standing by my side
You are always with me
You are always in my heart
I love you more with each passing moment.

MOTHER'S DAY

The greatest Mother's Day gift I ever
received
Was the birth of my only child
We didn't need a holiday to celebrate
As everyday was a gift.

Your last Mother's Day gift to me was to
start driving home
All I cared about was you making it home
safely
You made it safely home
Just not to me.

Another Mother's Day is approaching
Another year has passed
My heart is still broken
Tears still flow.

Fourteen Mother's Days have come and
gone
They all are just another day
Loving memories remain
Painful loss remains.

We didn't need a special day to celebrate
As every day was a gift
Those are the gifts that remain
Those are the gifts that last a life time.

You are my greatest gift.

GOOD INTENTIONS

People generally have good intentions
They do not know what to say
Making speech awkward
They cannot face your pain
They turn and walk away
They show sympathy
This does not help
They tell you what to do
They have no idea
They cannot know
They tell you they know how you feel
They do not have a clue.

Listening helps
A loving hug helps
Simply being with you helps
Not trying to make you feel better helps
Holding silent space helps.

People have good intentions.

THINGS THAT SHATTER

Glass shatters
Dishes shatter when they are dropped
Ice shatters
Mirrors shatter
They are all just things
They can be replaced.

Bones break and shatter
Bodies can be broken
Words can shatter the way you feel
Bad news can momentarily shatter your life
With time these things can heal.

The loss of a loved one
Devastates your life
Time moves forward
Your life continues on.

When you lose your child
Your life is shattered
Your heart is shattered
They cannot be fixed or replaced
You never heal or get over it
You learn how to cope
You learn how to manage life
Life continues on
Always shattered
Never the same.

THE FIRST SUMMER MORNING PADDLE

The sun has risen over the tree tops
The air is still cool and crisp
The sky is blue with white billowy clouds
The birds are beginning to sing their
morning symphony
The lake beckons me.

The water is like glass
My kayak slices through the water
Gliding with no resistance
Creating a whooshing noise
Blades of the paddle rhythmically enter and
leave the water
Creating a gentle splash
Ripples left behind in my wake
The lake beckons me.

Loons out fishing for breakfast
The first batch of baby Canada geese
swimming next to shore
Bugs flying just above the water's surface
Fish jumping for the flies
Dragonflies and butterflies keep me
company
The lake beckons me.

Reflections and shadows create magical
worlds on the water
The sun sparkles at my side
The dragonflies dance with their shadow
partners
To music only they can hear
The lake beckons me.

Alone on this lake

Thoughts simply flow through me
With peace and calm
Using my muscles to propel me forward
It is easy with no stress
Mindful meditation sets in
Connecting me to water, sky and air
Dissolving myself into all around me
The lake takes me home.

INNER LIGHT

The sky is an interesting mix of grey clouds
intermixed with some white ones
The lake is grey full of ripples yet the trees are a
plush green and perfectly still
It is a little eerie, but somehow it brings me
comfort
Reminds me that this too will pass and that I
have an inner light that still shines.

A totally grey morning
The sky is grey
The lake appears grey
Reflections are dark
Rain is predicted.

Rain cleans, refreshes and nourishes the
outside world
Allowing us to clean, refresh and nourish
our inside world
The air is heavy and calm
Bringing peace, quiet and comfort.

A hummingbird flies by
Leaving no trace
The glassy surface of the lake is disturbed
by a motor boat
Creating ripples
They hit the shore and bounce back
Creating chaos when the ripples meet each
other.

So much like life
There is stillness, peace and calm
That is disturbed by an external source
Creating chaos
Dissolving back into stillness
A gentle wind begins to blow
Creating movement on the water's surface.

We never know what the world will put in
front of us
We never know what will happen next
All we have is now

Which is constantly changing
All we can do is appreciate all that we have
As we flow along with life
Riding out the surface of the water
While always being the calm water beneath
the surface.

IINNER PEACE

Morning dawns to a stormy day
High winds
Heavy rain
White caps on the lake.

My house protects me from the storm
My inner peace is undisturbed
The gift of a day to stay inside
Doing inside chores.

The external world is in chaos
A nightclub shooting kills 49 people
The political world is frightening
Wildfires burn out of control
Torrential rains cause flooding
My inner peace is undisturbed.

A new day dawns
No rain
No wind
Calm waters
The lake awaits me.

Sitting in my kayak
Easily gliding on the water
The world's chaos cannot touch me here
My inner peace is undisturbed.

The east side of the lake is clear and calm
Rounding towards the north end
Ripples splash against my boat
My strokes stay rhythmic
Propelling me into the mist.

The mist engulfs me
My kayak and I disappear
I paddle forward
Trusting the lake
Becoming one with the mist
The mist protects me from the external
chaos
My inner peace is undisturbed.

The mist slowly rises
Clouds hover overhead
Hiding the sun's glow
The water and sky become united
I am here on the water
Yet connected with the sky above.

The boat ramp is in front of me
Time to end this paddle
Time to start the rest of my day.

The end of this day arrives
Bringing the gift of a magical sunset
Only the sounds of nature can be heard
The light of day fades
The dark of night surrounds me
My inner peace remains.

THE END OF JUNE

Where has time gone?
This month has flown by
This year is half over
Time truly has no meaning.

Sleep eluded me last night
Coyotes howling in the hills
Loons calling from the lake
The night sky is dark.

3:23am and I am wide awake
From my bed, the moon can be seen rising
A magical mist on the lake
A new day is dawning
The future awaits.

Daylight brightens the night sky
The hillsides hidden behind the fog
The mist rolls along the lake
Lifting from the opposite shore.

The sky turns to soft pink above the fog
Hummingbirds are active
Birds softly begin their early morning
symphony
The gifts of nature surround me
In perfection.

A fish jumps
Creating ripples on the glassy water
Life goes on
Simply flowing by
One day at a time.

The sun is starting to rise
The cycles of time
Less than two hours apart
This is human time.

Time has no meaning
As each new day arrives
Nature has no clocks
As it flows with perfection
Simply being.

A HEAVY MORNING

The day dawns slowly
The dark of night quietly flows into the light
of day
Clouds hiding the sun
The air is heavy with humidity
The sky is heavy with grey clouds
Fog lies heavily in the valleys
Not a breath of fresh air
The lake is like a mirror
Creating eerie reflections
The morning bird songs are quiet
A flock of geese silently float by
Two gulls land on the water
Hummingbirds flit around
If not for these winged beings
If not for my own breath
This world is perfectly still
It does not feel normal in this active
physical world
It feels like another realm
Where peace and stillness exist
There are times when these two realms
become one
Where all that exists are connected
Where there is no separation
Not today
Today that other realm is right here
I am sitting here in it
The heaviness of this morning
Brings lightness to my physical being
The spiritual realm totally engulfs my
humanness
I sit here alone
While connected to all there is

Evoking a knowingness of never being alone
Bringing peace and joy to every cell
Fueling my body
Empowering my soul
No chaos in my mind
This moment
This transition to a new day
Is absolutely perfect
There is no conflict or violence
The grey clouds are starting to lift
Glimmers of blue sky can be seen
Reflections on the water becoming clearer
Ripples appear on the opposite shore
Birds begin to sing
Dawn giving way to daylight
The gift of this morning will carry forward
into my day
The creation of all there is
The connection of all there is
Is real
Is palpable
Is available to all of us
All that is needed is to stop
To sit in the stillness
To disconnect from the chaos of this world
To come back to what is never lost
To come back to our own peace
To allow that peace to flow forward
Bringing peace to all there is.

Summer days at Grammy and Grampa's
beach house
The ride there in the back of the station
wagon
Bouncing on truck inner tubes
Playing in the sand
Building sand castles
Riding the waves on the inner tubes
Body surfing
Sitting on the big rocks as the tide comes in
Waves splashing over me
Turning rocks over when the tide is out
Looking for treasures from the sea
Home to the farm in time for dinner
Chores need to be done.

When I was 5
Grampa died just before Christmas
My mother said I could have the peanut
brittle I had bought him
Already wrapped and under the tree
Holidays were never the same
Summer days at the beach would be
different
My father buys the beach house
We now move there early in the spring
Staying till late in the fall.

It is an old three story cottage
Right on the beach
Full of old wood
Magical stairways
Hiding places
Huge claw foot bath tub

A shower with an overhead showerhead
That holds 12 people
An old wooden ice chest now electrified
So huge a large watermelon got lost in it
Large front and back porches
Flower boxes with red geraniums
Rose bushes along the side walk
A sun porch for those windy days.

My bedroom was in the corner on the
ocean side
A balcony off my parent's bedroom
beckoned me
Cots and sleeping bags were bought
My father and I slept out there
Feet towards the house
Heads towards the ocean
Cot turned next to the house when it rained
The ocean waves became my lullaby
The wind blew all my cares away
The stars magically carpeting the sky
The moon pulled my soul over the ocean
Peaceful undisturbed sleep
Beautiful dreams.

The sun starts to rise on the horizon's edge
Calling me from sleep
Bringing light to my eyes
Warmth to my face
Energy to my body
Nature's perfect alarm clock.

Darkness lingers
Everyone still asleep
My father and I quietly tiptoe our way
downstairs
Fresh coffee is brewed

Mine with milk and sugar
His is black
We sit together on the front porch step
Hands wrapped around our mugs
Shoulder to shoulder
Sometimes silent
Sometimes talking
He always answered my every question
We shared our plans for that day
As we watched a new day dawn
With the sun rising beyond and above the
ocean.

HOPE

What is Hope?
Webster's Dictionary says:
A feeling that what is wanted will happen
Desire accompanied by expectation.

Feelings come and go
Desires change
Expectations are met or not
What happens to Hope?

Hope creates dreams
Hope moves us forward
Hope propels us into the future
Hope is ever present.

Wants are just that
They are different from needs
Expectations create success or failure
Where does Hope fit in?

Needs are deeper than Hope
Having no expectations brings freedom
Accepting Reality is beyond Hope
Does Hope really exist?

Hope is fleeting
Hope can be lost
Hope is not real
Hope can change perspectives.

When Hope is gone
Life remains
Lives change
Disaster strikes

45

Yet, life goes on.

Every moment is new
The past is the foundation
The future has not arrived
The present moment is here now.

Is Hope real?
Hope can be found after it is lost
Hope can resurface when it has
disappeared
Hope can fade and shine again
Yes, Hope exists and lives on.

THE MOON

Two o'clock in the morning
Darkness surrounds me
My body is warm under blankets
My bed holds me in comfort
It is not time to get up
Yet I am beckoned to rise.

The house is filled with moonlight
The moon is visible in the western sky
It's light reflecting on the still waters
A spectacular sight
Creating a path
That one cannot physically walk
Yet clearly connecting me to what lies
beyond.

No human sounds
No human light
Wrapped in a blanket
I sit in the silent night
Watching the moon move through the sky.

As the moon nears the mountains
The path of light diminishes
The moon reaches the mountain top
Individual trees can be seen
The moon sinks behind the mountain
Its light is still visible
Then slowly disappears
Leaving total darkness.

The moon has disappeared from my sight
Yet it still exists
The sun has not risen into my sight

Yet it still exists
This is the natural flow
The moon rises out of darkness
Brilliantly shining its light
Then it fades away leaving darkness behind
While bringing light to another place.

The natural cycle of the moon
Reflects the flow of life
We are born into this world out of darkness
We shine brightly for a time
We disappear back into the darkness
We can no longer be seen
Yet we are never gone
Just out of sight.

The path of light keeps us connected
As we hold sacred space
Knowing we will be seen again.

HALLOWEEN

Sitting in a stranger's house
Staying with people you barely know
You wake at your normal hour of 3:00 am
Finally finding your way downstairs at 5:30.

The house is dark
All is quiet
Finding light switches along the way
The kitchen awaits.

Coffee is brewed
A comfy chair beckons you
Facing a big picture window
Today is Halloween.

This is the time of year when the veil
between the two worlds is thinnest
It is a time of honoring and celebrating
those that walk beyond where we can see
Children today go trick or treating
Dressing in costumes
Knocking on doors
Getting candy
They are innocent to anything beyond.

Daylight slowly arrives
The sky lightens
Dark clouds can be seen
Trees appear black
Their branches moving with the wind
Light reflecting off the water
It is like an old black and white picture
Being framed by the window.

The eye drifts back to inside the house
There is color, warmth and light
Other people are still sleeping
Life still exists as this new day dawns.

Thoughts drift to life beyond this physical
world
Where we cannot see or touch
Yet we know exists
Today is a day to remember
To connect
To reach out to where we do not walk
To feel the unconditional love in our hearts
To know these two worlds are truly all one
To know that life exists beyond what the
eye can see.

More daylight
Bringing color to the outside world
Definition of trees, grass, rocks and hillsides
Leaves gently float by
Ripples on the water.

This is the physical world where we exist
The contrast between the two worlds is
clear
Yet another world exists
A world where connections can be made
Only a breath away
Yet so far away.

Thank you Halloween for the gift of bringing
these two worlds together
For all to connect and celebrate in their
own way
A new day has dawned
Life goes on.

50

THE SUPER MOON

Two nights ago the almost full moon rose in
a crystal clear sky
Brilliant, huge, powerful, magical, so close
to this earth
Creating light and shadows throughout the
night.

As the moon moved through the sky
Shadows moved on the ground
As the moon neared the mountains
Ridgelines and individual trees could be
seen
The reflection on the lake was like a golden
path
The water was like glass
Not a ripple to be seen.

Time passes as the moon sinks behind the
mountains
Leaving darkness till a new day dawns.

Last night the full moon rose into a cloudy
sky
It's brilliance still present
Yet hidden
Creating rings of color through the clouds
A mystical circular rainbow from above.

The moon moves through the sky
The clouds also move through the sky
There is always light in the dark sky
Sometimes the moon is clear
Sometimes it is hidden
Sometimes creating shapes that only the

imagination can capture.

The moon is always present
Bringing light to the dark night.

What is light, dark, time?
These are words that we as humans have
given to the natural flow of existence
The earth and moon are solid
They can be seen, touched and explained
through science
We as humans need words to communicate
Words bring meaning to things beyond our
grasp
Yet words have no effect on existence.

We are so small
Like a grain of sand on the beach
Our time in this physical world
Is like a blink of an eye
When compared to infinity
There is so much more beyond what the
eye can see.

The moon brings light to the dark of night
The dark of night hides the boundaries that
day light allows us to see
Life exists beyond these boundaries.

Darkness is like a cloud we walk in during
times of pain and suffering
This darkness feels all-consuming and heavy
Yet when compared to the darkness of the
night
It is like that grain of sand on the beach.

The darkness of night absorbs our individual

darkness
The two become one
As all existence merges together
Eternal connections are possible
Beyond where the eye can see.

I sit here in the darkness at 3 o'clock in the
morning
Watching the super moon move through
the night sky
Bringing light to the darkness
Creating magical shapes with clouds
Reflecting mystical colors
Letting me know I am not alone.

As I glance up to the moon from my paper
The shape I see is an angel
The moon in the center where the heart
resides
A clear sign from beyond
That I am not alone.

Thank you Kenny, my son
For eternal connections
For unconditional love
And your guiding light.

The moon has now disappeared
Leaving me in total darkness
Connecting me to all that exists
Beyond what the eye can see.

Good bye for now
Till I see you again.

2016
BLESSING

As I sit here overlooking Lake Parker
The water looks more like the ocean
Two loons have landed to rest on their flight
south
It is snowing so hard I can barely see the
other side of the lake
Yet, above the snow
There is beautiful blue sky
Pink and white billowy clouds
I have never seen another afternoon like
this.

As I reflect on this past year
This afternoon is symbolic of the year gone
by
Violence erupts all over the world
Natural disasters continue one after the
other
Tragedy strikes without warning
The political world has been shocked into
reality.

We have a choice
We can react to the events
causing more unrest
Or we can choose for peace
We can rise above the turmoil of the
surface
Like the blue sky holding clouds.

The holiday season can be chaotic
Yet it can also be a time for slowing down
Being with friends and family

Sharing memories with joy, laughter and
love in our hearts.

As this year comes to a close
My wish to all of you is to maintain calm
To be at peace
To hold onto the unconditional love that is
never lost
And to cherish the good times.

THE FIRST DAY OF
2017

My clock said 1:00 when I woke from a
deep sleep
This was the first hour of the first day of
2017
Another year has slipped by seemingly
unnoticed
A new year is beginning
What will it bring?
I have no idea!
Right at this moment in time, I need to go
back to sleep
There is a chill in the air
My bed is warm and comfy
No stars can be seen
All is quiet, not even the sound of wind
Sleep comes easily at this hour
4:00 o'clock arrives
Is it time to start this first day of the new
year?
No, not yet, that can wait
Time to simply let my never ending
thoughts flow through me
Lying on my right side, I am facing the wall
Lying on my left side, the bedroom door is
open
Lying on my back, I can look out two
windows
The wall represents obstacles we face in life
They can block us from moving forward
The bedroom door represents the known
We are comfortable here as we know our
way around
The windows represent the unknown

It is still dark yet I can see the white snow
and the silhouettes of the trees
I cannot see any stars
The moon would be on the other side of the
house at this time of year.
It was snowing when I went to bed
But I cannot tell if the snow is still falling
I have no idea what this new day will bring
Yet, I trust that dawn will arrive
Bringing light for all to see as the darkness
fades
These three visions are symbolic of life
We can stay stuck behind the walls
We can walk comfortably in the familiar
Or we can bravely walk out into the
unknown
How will I walk into this new year once my
feet hit the floor?
Letting my every thought and emotion flow
through me while snuggling deep in my
warm, comfy bed
I make a decision
It is time for my feet to feel the floor
For my body to feel the chill of the morning
To allow my eyes to adjust to the darkness
To venture into this new year, into the
unknown
To discover what lies ahead
To let nothing hold me back
To trust my future lies ahead
To allow this first day of this new year to
unfold perfectly
As I walk into this next year of my life.

CLARITY

Am I a seeker?
I never thought of myself that way
Other's see me that way.

What is a seeker?
It is just a word
It has many meanings
There are seekers of knowledge
        Scientific discoveries
        Medical answers and cures
        Explorers
        Spirituality
        Enlightenments
        Seekers of shells
To me, a seeker is someone always looking
for something.

Sitting here in a friend's house in Rehoboth,
Delaware
Drinking hot, strong coffee
Watching this new day dawn
Overlooking the bay at the mouth of the
ocean
My heart is at peace
My mind is at rest
My soul is home.

There were lights across the bay
That I could see when it was dark
They have now disappeared into the light of
day
The sea birds were invisible
They are now entertaining me
The wind is calm

The water is like glass
The sun continues to rise
Bringing changing light
The clouds have a life all of their own
At a glance, everything remains the same
Yet when you really observe
Nothing remains the same
Everything continually changes
Everything naturally flows
Unfolding in perfect harmony
Absolutely perfect just as it is
As I sit here in peace
Without a care in the world
My mind can watch the movie of my life to
this point.

Was I a seeker?
Probably so
Have all my experiences made me who I am
today?
Most definitely
Have all my journeys brought me here?
Obviously
Do I know how the movie will end?
No
What I do know is that perfection lies within
Peace lies within
Clarity lies within
All we have to do is stop seeking
Look within
And allow life to dawn in perfect harmony
Exactly as it is.

WHO AM I

I can list the things I have done
I can list the things I do
I can list my qualities
But are these lists who I am?
No!

Sitting on a friend's lounge in Rehoboth,
Delaware
I am free
I am comfortable
I simply am
I am an early riser
She sleeps in
This is the gift of quiet mornings.

The first morning
I could see the lights across the bay come
on one by one
As the day dawned
The water became visible
Sea birds entertained me
Clouds appeared
Everything around me unfolded in slow
motion
Houses could be seen
The bay opening to the ocean was there
Sun glistened on the water
Every moment was perfect exactly as it was
Nothing seemed to change
Yet change was constant
Nothing to do except sit and watch
Peace within me
Peace surrounded me.

The second morning
Day dawned with clarity
The moon was visible
Tail lights of cars leaving from across the
bay
Appeared then disappeared
The water was like glass
Then ripples found their way to the shore
The shapes of clouds quickly morphed
The jet streams from airplanes
Appeared, then dissolved into the sky
Fog started to roll in from the ocean
Rain began falling.

This third morning
Greeted me with thick fog
Day light slowly grew from the darkness
Bird songs were muffled
Visibility was only to the water's edge
Darkness turned to deep grey
Turning an earthly shade
Becoming lighter yet still existing
Seagulls were flying along the water's edge
The fog became less dense
Nothing seemed to change
Yet change was constant
Nothing to do except sit and watch
Peace within me
Peace surrounding me.

Tomorrow, the fourth morning
I will leave this piece of heaven
To continue my journey onward
These mornings are just like life
Never knowing what will come
A picture perfect dawn
A dawn full of clarity

A foggy dawn
Every moment changing
Unfolding before my eyes
Peace within me
Peace surrounding me
I am peace.

THE JOURNEY CONTINUES

This leg of my journey is coming to an end
It is the second stop on a month long trip
Heading south to escape the grey, cold
winter days of Vermont
Have not traveled far enough to reach the
warmth and sunshine
Yet my heart is warm and overflowing with
love
Staying with friends
They welcomed me with love and
understanding
They opened their homes to me with
generous hospitality
They shared their lives with heartfelt,
honest conversation
They were tour guides.

These are the things that make a difference
in people's lives.

This fourth morning in Rehoboth, Delaware
Greeted me with the moon moving through
the darkness
Giving way to all-encompassing light
The sky is filled with blue and grey clouds
The water still grey and calm
The sun is rising but from where I sit
It is still hidden.

No two mornings are the same
No two places are the same
Countless days lie ahead
Many places to see
Many miles to travel

The past does not hold me back
The future awaits
Never knowing what I will see
Yet knowing it will be perfect just as it is
My heart feels warm and overflowing with
love
This is what connects us all
This is what allows us to appreciate the
natural beauty always surrounding us
This is what keeps us moving forward
Into every new day
Never knowing what lies ahead
The journey continues.

WHAT DO I DO

I am loving Sun City and could see myself
living here
I have made an offer on a house
But no final contract signed yet
We shall see.

I am not attached to the outcome
My intuition is that she will not sign my final
offer
I took a leap of faith and if it works, great
If it doesn't, there will be another place for
me.

Need to get out for some fresh air and
exercise.
Will then do some repacking to get ready to
leave for Punta Gorda tomorrow
My journey continues
Being here has made me realize that I can
have a life beyond grief
I completely feel like an empty container
Waiting to see what will fill me up.

ALWAYS HOME

Where is home?
Most people think home is where you live
Some people think it is where you were
born
There is a saying that home is where the
heart is
So, where is home?

Home is more than a place
Home is more than a feeling
Home is a connection with where you are
If time has no meaning,
Then the past is over
The future does not exist yet
All we have is now
Is this home?

Home is being with friends who welcome
you
With love and understanding
Who share open and honest conversations.

Home is watching a new day dawn with a
sunrise
And at the end of the day watching the
sunset
Home is sitting in silence while simply being
in peace
Listening to the bird's symphonies
Allowing the birds to entertain you
Watching the fog roll in and out
Watching the shapes and colors of clouds
morph

Watching dolphins play in the ocean from
the top of a lighthouse you have climbed
Eating lunch at a funky little restaurant on
the ocean's edge under the sun that
reminds you of the islands
Walking on a beach with your feet in the
water
Seeing Manatees for the first time
Coming face to face with a sleeping alligator
Riding bikes with a group of friends
Playing pickleball
Swimming
Sitting in a hot tub at the end of the day
Seeing the shape of an angel in the clouds
Seeing a rainbow spot in the sky as the sun
rises above the ocean
Walking the beach as the sun sets and the
moon rises
Feeling the power of the full moon as it
glistens over the ocean
Finding a broken shell in the shape of a
heart
Seeing the snow falling even in the darkness
of night
Watching snowflakes fall as each one
dances in the wind
Taking time to feel connected to all there is,
has ever been and will ever be
Being one with the beauty of nature that
surrounds us.

These are the places where home resides
Like a turtle carrying its shell
Home is within us every moment
We can never leave home
Nor can we return home
We are always home.

RAINBOWS

One wintry day, I was driving north during a
snow storm
There would be periods of whiteouts
Then periods of sunshine
One could see the next whiteout up ahead
The winds were screaming
Clouds were flying by
Going through mountain passes
The clouds were so low that visibility was
zero.

Every few miles there would be a rainbow
Some were full spectrum
Some were barely visible
Some were double
There was one that was a complete circle
Totally engulfing my car
It was magical and mysterious
This was a first for me.

I wondered if other drivers were paying
attention
If other drivers even cared about this
natural phenomenon
My mind went to wondering about
rainbows
Scientists have an explanation
Mystics have their own interpretation
Lepricons bring magic to them.

Every rainbow I see
Is meant just for me
They are brilliant, beautiful and perfect for
just a short time
Now I see them, now I don't

Rainbows after the rain
Rainbows during a snowstorm
Rainbows during the sunrise
Rainbows during the sunset
A rainbow in the shape of a ball
A rainbow in a complete circle with no
beginning and no ending
Rainbow colors in clouds.

Driving across Montana, I was the only car
on the road
A double rainbow appeared in front of me
And a double rainbow appeared behind me
At that moment, my entire presence was
ablaze with color.

Rainbows have special meaning to each
person who sees one
All you have to do is pay attention
To be present in their glory, color and
magnificence
To stop for a moment and rest in their
natural beauty
To hear the messages they are whispering
to you.

For me, rainbows are a work of art
Building magical bridges
Between this physical world and the
spiritual world beyond our grasp
They give me a moment to connect where I
cannot walk
To see beyond what is right in front of me
To remind me that unity exists
That life is eternal
That nothing is beyond my reach
Rainbows are a special gift
Brought to me from far away.
69

Meditation brings me to that place of
stillness
The place where my authentic self resides
The place of peace within
Beyond all thoughts, feelings and emotions
Where there is no judgement or criticism
Nothing is wrong, nothing is broken
Everything is absolutely perfect exactly as it
is.

This is the place where deep healing
happens
Where pain and suffering ceases to exist
Where scabs fall away from wounds
Where time stands still
Where strength and courage erupt
The root of awareness.

Awareness when the external world pulls
me out
Awareness to return
Awareness when thoughts, feelings and
emotions tug on my heart
Awareness pulls me back
Awareness when I feel broken
Awareness brings me back to perfection.

Awareness brings me back to stillness
Stillness allows my mind, body and spirit to
heal
Healing fills the holes that death created
The holes are filled with eternal presence
Where I am united with all there is, all there
was and all there will ever be

70

Where loneliness no longer exists
Where all my wounds are healed
Making me whole
Where I have become friends with my
authentic self
Where my son's eternal life continues to
walk.

This physical body is now ready to go forth
Beyond the boundaries created by human
expectations
To break through those walls of fear
Opening to new experiences
One hand is held by my friend, my authentic
self
One held is held by my son in eternity
I shall never walk alone again.

THE TRIP

What is this trip about?
It was planned with a purpose
That purpose still exists
Though the details fell apart
Reaching out for connections
Being held in loving hands
Sitting in sacred space
It is the journey that is important
Not the end result.

INTEGRATION

Last week, while on a conference call
The group was asked what their divine
purpose is
To speak from their authentic self
Not from their mind.

My initial thought was, this is easy, I know
this
Then I sat in silence while listening deeply
to the others
So many more thoughts came flooding into
my mind
I would take a deep breath and return to
that silent place within.

My mind came up with all kinds of words
Yet none resonated with my inner knowing
The question then arose within me
Do I really know my divine purpose?
There was nothing there, no answers.

I could not find words to share
What I was feeling was beyond words
Yet words are how we as humans
communicate
Struggling to find words to express
something that is beyond words
I finally surrendered and remained silent.

The call ended
We all said bye, love you and see you next
week
My pondering soul needed to understand
To answer the question for myself
To return to that place of undisturbed
peace.

My mind, body and soul simply sat with the
question
I never remember a time where I felt like I
belonged here
I would escape to my private inner
sanctuary
When the external world became
overwhelming
To my private place that I shared with no
one.

I could never define where here was
I just knew it wasn't where I was.
I never felt like any place I was living
was home
This feeling led to many different jobs
Too many moves
Too many wonderful experiences.

My life became one great adventure
With an eclectic background
Always moving from one thing to another
Never letting much grass grow under my
feet.

Along came marriage
A child
Living the American Dream
Then my whole world was pulled out from
underneath me
That all too familiar feeling of not belonging
here came flooding back
This time I knew why
Not wanting to be here
Yet remaining here
Not knowing how to be here
Yet here I was.

As time went on
I had one foot in this world
One foot in the spirit world
I didn't belong in either place
While struggling to discover how to be here.

I thought my divine purpose was to be of
service
To be here now
To love life
To bring peace to the world
To be a wounded healer.

If this were true
Why could I not find these words to share
I thought just being me was enough
Listening to other answers
I knew there was more
But what was my answer?

Some days later, my friend offered me a
massage
We both fell into that place of stillness
That place of connectedness
That deep place within
Where unconditional love resides
Where deep healing flows freely
Where we are all perfect.

As she was working on freeing up my right
hip
Things started to come together
I finally knew where here was
I finally knew where home is.

Here is this physical world
Home is the spirit world

I am here now
My divine purpose will be fulfilled
When I reach home.

HOME

They say Home is where the Heart is
Home is so much more
The Heart is so much more.

The heart is the first sign of human life
The heart gives us life
Till it doesn't
Then eternal life begins.

Home is that silent place within
Where all that we are exists
Where knowledge is held
Where love resides
Where light burns brightly.

As a young child
I would retreat to this inner silent place
It was my private sanctuary
Where I was safe
Where I would find answers
Where comfort held me.

I have been called a seeker
I would ask: A seeker of what?
There were never any answers.

A life time of seeking for a place to belong
A home where I can peacefully rest
Led me to escape the cold, grey winter days
In search of warmth and sunshine
To the south
Seeking a new place to call home.

This trip was an unfamiliar journey

Yet felt comfortable and right
4,000 miles on my car
Always staying with friends
Experiencing different life styles.

I simply went with the flow
From one place to another
Feeling like a camillian
Fitting in everywhere
Socializing with everyone
Having fun
I could live anywhere.

Could I make one of these places home?
There are pros and cons to every place
The one thing that never changed
Was my private inner sanctuary.

It has always been with me
Sometimes I would forget to visit
But it never left me
Always present
Always available
Always waiting for me to return.

That secret inner sanctuary is home
Everywhere else is just another place
Being home brings freedom
Freedom to live any place
Freedom to be at peace
Freedom to be here now
Freedom to be present.

I am already home
In my private inner sanctuary.

THE LAKE

The Lake, always present
In summer it is free flowing water
In winter there is ice on the surface
With water beneath.

The summer allows water activities
The winter allows for different activities
The lake is like a four season resort
Always offering something to do.

In summers the water can be like glass
Have gentle ripples
White caps
Or actual waves.

Mist will rise from the surface
The water is a reflecting glass
Beautiful fall colors
The surrounding mountains and trees
Creating shadows
Reflecting sunrises and sunsets
The moon creating a pathway to the stars.

Fog can be so thick you cannot see
Yet it can be brilliantly clear or dark
You can see fish swimming
Weeds growing
And bugs floating on the surface.

Water birds swim and float
Diving for food
Turtles napping on the shore
Going for a swim to cool off
Loons float in care-free harmony

Building nests in the tall reeds
The Lake creates a life all unto itself.

In winter the water freezes
Snow accumulates on the surface
Wind picks up the new fallen snow
Creating white-outs
Snow designs develop
Constantly changing
No two are the same.

Sometimes it is snowing so hard
The opposite shore is hidden
There is no distinction of land and water
As the snow builds up along the banks
On calm days, the snow is perfectly flat
No visible signs of disturbance
No human has touched the surface.

The lake sings to us
Usually in an ethereal tone
The ice has its own vibration
Sounding more like a drum
The sound draws your attention
Connecting human senses with natural
occurrences.

Earlier this winter
During a February thaw
The ice started to melt
Water beneath
Water above
Large cracks forming as the ice broke apart
Water becoming a reflecting pond.

Depths of winter return
Temperatures dropping to below zero

Snow falling
The winter lake returns.

The Lake is a gentle reminder of life
Always present
Always changing
Unpredictable
Never knowing what will be next.

SPRING FULL MOON

The power of the full moon drew me from
bed at 4:00 this morning
No need to turn on lights to see my way
Rising night-time temperatures
Allowed the house to stay warm
Insulated shades rolled up
The full moon is right there
Taking my breath away
Drawing my energy towards it
A brilliantly beautiful golden circle
In the dark night sky
Its light reflecting off the frozen
snow-covered lake
Creating a path directly to me.

Slowly the moon sinks toward the
mountains
Slipping behind clouds
Drifting from sight
Day light begins to soften the sky
Clouds turning a soft, gentle pink
The sun rising higher in the sky
Shines on the mountain tops
A strip of light across the frozen lake
Can now be seen
Shadows being created.

The sky turns blue
Clouds turn a billowy white
The shadow of my house
Surrounded by the shadows of trees
The shadows are an extension of my house
Protecting me from the outside elements
The gift of this new day

Freely given
Received through my eyes
My eyes are the gateway to natural beauty
Unfolding before me
In absolute perfection.

Thank you moon
For this gift
Reminding me how easily everything flows
If we simply pay attention.

CAMDEN, MAINE

The rocky coast of Maine has not changed
The years of my life have changed the
person I am
The ocean calls me home
The sounds and sights sooth my soul
Bringing peace, calm and joy into my
awareness
Waves crash against the rocks
With unharnessed power
Islands off the shore
Letting us know there is more
A never ending horizon
Flowing into the sky
A single loon appears
The tide comes in
Creating islands from the rocks
The night sky begins to arrive
Are we seeing dark clouds in the last of light
Or white clouds in the early dark night sky
The answer lies in your perception
Does it really matter
In this present moment surrounded by
natural beauty

Awareness of all there is engulfs my being
Everything morphs together
I cease to exist
Complete unity is all there is
Darkness sets in
Daylight fades away
Nighttime arrives
The sound of waves and rain drift through
sleep
Daylight calls me to wake

The rain is heavier
Thick fog surrounds me
Ocean sounds still exist
A ringing buoy can be heard
Fog slowly drifts away
Rocks become visible
The ocean still present
Birds can be seen
The islands reappear
Rain, wind and currents create art work on
the water
My eyes track the sound of the buoy
bobbing as a warning signal
The fog rolls back in
hiding what once I could see
Sounds become louder
The tide turns
Crashing into the rocks
Splashing above them
Water covering what I could see only
moments before
How magical the ocean is
Reminding me how quickly things change
The ocean has a life all of its own
Always present
Always changing
Always calling me home.

THE OCEAN
Popham Beach, Maine

Why the ocean calls me home:

The ocean is
Always present
Always changing
Always there
All we have to do is show up.

Sometimes the ocean is full of fury
Sometimes it is calm
The ocean holds life
With its own rhythm
The ocean brings treasures to shore
Beach stones
Drift wood
Sea glass
Shells, some whole and some are broken
It doesn't matter
They are all perfect exactly as they are
I see them and walk on
Leaving them for someone else
I have enough
I don't need any more.

Waves form out of the sea
They build till they crest and break
The white wash comes to shore till it thins
and returns to the sea
Distant shoals out on the horizon
Waves crash against them
Splashing and spraying water upwards to
the sky
Now you see them
Now you don't

As they return to the sea.

Sea birds fly overhead signing to me
Or float on the water's surface
Drifting with the current
A seal rises out of the depths
Faces me as if to say hello, welcome home.

Wind blows all around me
Sun warms my face
Sand under my feet
Supports my every step
Footprints left in the sand
Disappear under the waves
Footprints left behind say I was here
But have now joined the sea as I walked on
Here one moment
Yet not the next.

The ocean is never silent
It can roar and pound
Or gently lap the shore
The ocean noise drowns out my thoughts
The ocean's power heals my being
The ocean's flow cleanses my soul
The ocean draws me to a place where I can
stop
And watch the magical sea
For as long as I need
The external chaos ceases to exist
When I dissolve into the sea.

Home is within each of us
Always present
Always changing
Always there
All we have to do is show up and gently pay
attention.

87

YOU CAN NEVER GO BACK

The older we get
The more memories we have
Some good
Some we would prefer to forget
Our minds like to replay our memories
We can physically take a trip down memory
lane
Only to realize that what we remember
May not be exactly right
May have changed
May not be what we thought it was.

We may have dreamed of returning
Only to discover that once we return it was
only a dream
We were holding on to something we did
not have
We are no longer the person who created
the dream
We have stepped away from the past
As we walked into the future
And rest in the present moment.

How pleasant to take a trip down memory
lane
How precious to have sweet dreams
How wonderful to simply watch our future
unfold before us
Without getting stuck in the past.

TRANSITIONS

In honor of Sivadasa

The weather pattern this spring
Has been grey, cold and rainy
This is just a pattern
Something out of our control
Not at all personal
Yet, exactly what this corner of the world
needed at this time
The natural flow
Allows beauty to unfold
We don't have to do anything
Other than show up
Be present
And appreciate what is right in front of us
When we are patient
Patterns change
Transitions happen
Sometimes unnoticed.

The rain finally stopped
The air became still
The lake as smooth as glass
Reflecting the surrounding mountains
The trees are lush
With the new crisp green growth
Awakening from the dormant winter
months
The sky still holds thick clouds
No longer full of rain
No blue to be seen
Just pure light
There is peace and calm surrounding me
A lone loon pops up right in front of me
As if to say Hello

I am still here

Reminding me how perfect this present
moment is
He spreads his wings and shakes off the
water
Then comfortably settles back down
Simply resting
Simply being
Absolutely perfect
Then he dives and disappears
To surface in another place.

Time ticks by
The day transitions to evening
As the sun approaches the mountains
Its brilliant light radiates through the thick
clouds
Letting me know it is still there
Even when my eyes cannot see it
It slowly drifts behind the mountains
The sky becomes a blaze of brilliant colors
Constantly changing
Being reflected on the water
Then slowly the colors sink behind the
mountains
Following the sun
Gently allowing the darkness to fall around
me.

A new day dawns
With soft grey light
The promise of sun is clear
Heavy mist floats on the water
Its tops like many fingers touching the sky
It rises higher than the mountains
Connecting this physical world with all that

is beyond
Slowly drifting toward the north
It eventually disappears
Leaving behind a glorious day
Full of sunshine
Natural beauty
Not a cloud in the sky
No wind
Clear, calm, peace
Absolutely perfect.

This gift of the ending of one day and the dawning of another was from my friend, Sivadasa, as he transitions to another world. His light will always shine brightly. His beauty will remain. He will always be here. His love will never fade.

As Bereaved Parents, we will always walk with a hole in our hearts. We would gladly give anything just to see our children one more time. We know this is not possible, until the day that we join them, but our hearts still want it. As a result, we all look for signs or messages that our children are still present. These signs are always surrounding us, if we are receptive and pay attention. Through my meditation practice and studies, I have come to believe that we are all always connected. I feel Kenny's presence most strongly in nature.

I received notice that a dear friend only had hours to live. I prayed for him and prayed to Kenny to be there for him. Then, the sun started to set and the next day dawned. I sat and wrote TRANSITIONS just as my friend was taking his last breaths.

ABOUT THE AUTHOR

Ann Lindner was living the American Dream in central Vermont when her life was shattered by the sudden death of her only child in 2002. She has now retired and lives on an idyllic lake in the heart of Vermont's Northeast Kingdom. Throughout her life, Ann always found comfort in nature and with animals. In 2009 she learned how to meditate, Soon thereafter, she found her way to Spain to study meditation at a deeper level and became a meditation teacher. She now travels to meditation retreats, teaching meditation and presenting meditation workshops at National Bereaved Parent Conferences.

Made in the USA
San Bernardino, CA
11 October 2018